Ernesto KOEHLER

35 EXERCISES FOR FLUTE OPUS 33

(Book 1)

Edited by Carol Wincenc

Contents

Page 2 — № 1. Allegro moderato — *mf dolce*

Page 3 — № 2. Allegretto — *mf energico*

Page 4 — № 3. Allegro — *mf*

Page 5 — № 4. Allegretto vivo — *p*

Page 6 — № 5. Allegretto — *f marziale*

Page 7 — № 6. Allegro — *f deciso*

Page 8 — № 7. Allegretto — *p*

Page 9 — № 8. Allegro moderato — *p grazioso*

Page 10 — № 9. Allegretto — *mf martellato*

Page 11 — № 10. Moderato — *f risoluto*

Page 12 — № 11. Allegro molto — *mf ben legato*

Page 13 — № 12. Moderato — *p*

Page 14 — № 13. Andantino — *p a guisa di Barcarola*

Page 14 — № 14. Allegro — *f*

Page 16 — № 15. Moderato — *f risoluto*

Production: Joe Derhake
Covers: Cynthia Gillette
Cover photo: Christian Steiner
Music engraving: Maria Cook

LAUREN KEISER
MUSIC PUBLISHING

15 EASY EXERCISES

Edited by: Carol Wincenc

ERNESTO KOEHLER
Op. 33, Book I

№ 1. **Allegro moderato**

№ 2. **Allegretto**

№ 3. Allegro

№ 4. Allegretto vivo

№ 5. Allegretto

№ 6. Allegro

№ 7. Allegretto

№ 8. **Allegro moderato**

№ 9. Allegretto

№ 10. Moderato

№ 11. Allegro molto

№ 12. Moderato

№ 13. Andantino

№ 14. Allegro

№ 15. Moderato

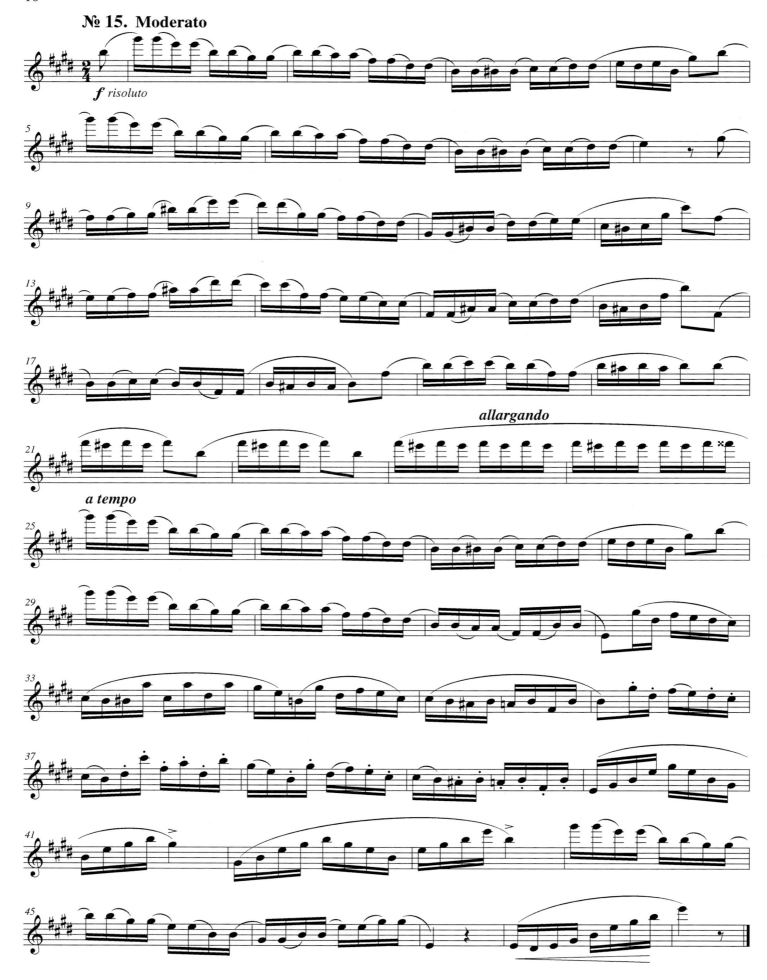